All Scripture references taken from the KJV of the Holy Bible, unless otherwise indicated.

THE KEYS TO YOUR NEW HOUSE:
AND EVERYTHING ELSE

Dr. Marlene Miles

Freshwater Press 2025

Freshwaterpress9@gmail.com

ISBN: 978-1-967860-50-0

Paperback Version

Table of Contents

THE KEYS to Your New House: *and Everything Else*

Freshwater

Dreams About Keys

This book is about keys—those that unlock doors and it's about keys that make things happen and create harmony in things that do happen.

I've had several dreams about keys and perhaps you have as well. Remember, God talks to you in a unique way, so be sure to get Biblical, Christian dream interpretation. The same dream can mean different things to different folks. Your dream can mean something for right now and something different, or something more five years from now. God is deep like that.

Keys can mean authority, or freedom. Those keys could be to unlock the prison doors for example. Keys symbolize power among other things. Deliverance, for yourself or for whom you pray.

But we are not just here to talk about dreams today. In this book we will share about things in the natural and in the spirit that are spiritual, but they are not night visions or dreams.

I want to talk about the keys to your house – the one you live in and the one that you are a part of, such as the HOUSE of ...... whatever your last name is. The House of the Williams family, the House of the Jones family, whatever family you are a part of. That house. The name of your father's house. Those keys.

Who holds the keys? Who holds the keys or has the most authority in your bloodline. Is it you?

Regarding your father's house, your father, if he is still alive, praise God. If not, may the Lord rest his soul. Now what he did with those keys determines a lot about your life and your family's life.

I will give you the keys of the kingdom of heaven; and whatever you bind on earth shall have been bound in heaven, and whatever you loose on earth shall have been loosed in heaven. (Matthew 16:19)

I dreamed one night many, many years ago that I met my grandfather – whom I had never met, as he had predeceased me. But I knew him only by pictures I had seen in old family photo. In the dream he handed me a piece of paper with four numbers written on it.

1818

I prayed about these numbers and sought to know what it meant or why it was given to me. That was not the year he was born or anything else like that, so it was perplexing. I worked on the meaning of this dream for several days and then I found it:

Verily I say unto you, Whatsoever ye shall bind on earth shall be bound in heaven: and whatsoever ye shall loose on earth shall be loosed in heaven. (Mark 18:18)

That's what started me into spiritual warfare, binding and loosing many years ago. Thank God for that dream and

7

interpretation. So, it was my grandfather, not my father that made me notice these keys – the LORD gave the keys, but my grandfather shed light on them.

Even though I never met him, my grandfather was a very spiritual man from what I had heard. One night he dreamed of what man to go to see and what amount of money to take to buy a certain parcel of land. He got up the next morning and did just as his dream directed and bought the land that my family all lived on, and still have houses and family members on that large parcel of land.

Dreams are how God can speak to us.

Your Father's House

Your father. Your father's father and his father before him, they had the keys to your life by the power to bind and *loose*. Prayerfully, they were in Christ, and they *loosed* good things into the family and bloodline into the house of whatever your last name is, and bound and removed unacceptable things.

This is a major role of the priest of a house, the family: Priesting over a bloodline. The role of the father is not to yell and bully the family. He is not to appoint himself as king and demand worship and service from everyone in the house. His job is to *priest* over that house. His role is to be speaking Godly words, declarations and encouragement and exhortation over the family and watching and praying and looking out for the family both physically and spiritually.

In a family line where the older ones are going on to Glory or may have already gone on to Glory, looking at who is left – who is the oldest male now in your bloodline? Who is the patriarch of the bloodline? Is he a good priest over your bloodline, or not? Is he God-approved, or has God appointed someone else? It doesn't have to be the oldest person although it often is.

Who is the oldest female, the matriarch of that family? Those two positions hold a lot of authority. It is not the bossy controlling power freak that we may see on shows like *Law and Order,* although the role can be perverted if not done God's way, but instead by manipulation and control. The patriarch and matriarch are the priests of the house. Their role is to bless and teach and speak what is allowed or disallowed in that family spiritually. It is to handle, hold and disseminate the spiritual legacy of that family.

Pray for those people in that position in your family. If you are one of those people, may the Lord empower you to allow what God allows, and reject what is not of God for all of those under your auspices. Be a good leader, a Godly priest over what you have been given charge over, and give respect and honor where it is due. Amen.

Whether you are the oldest, or the oldest remaining, in your own household, in your own life, you are right now directing not only your own life, but also directing the lives of your children by binding and *loosing*. You are impacting your spouse's life, your marriage, your family, your business, and many other things by your binding and *loosing*. These keys are the keys to everything. Everything you do, say, every action impacts your own life as well as the life of your family, your marriage and your children and far into the future. You may think that is a lot of responsibility, and it is. It is a lot of power. We think we want power? We have it. If we are not fully aware that we have it, it can be lost, stolen, or abused. It could be weaponized to hurt a family or a bloodline instead of blessing that bloodline.

The Warfare

Spiritual warfare? You may say no one charged you to do that. No one gave you a piece of paper with 1818 written on it. You may say that you aren't into all that loud praying? Well, sometimes you have to be. The kingdom of heaven suffereth violence and the violent take it by force.

And from the days of John the Baptist until now the kingdom of heaven suffereth violence, and the violent take it by force.
(Matthew 11:12)

However, whether you are into spiritual warfare or not, any loud, dynamic praying, we still bind and *loose* all day long. We bind and *loose* at night while we are asleep because the spirit man is not asleep; he never sleeps. We bind and *loose* in our dreams and that is why things come to us in our dream; the devil wants to trick us into agreements at night while we are asleep.

We bind and *loose*, sometimes without saying a word. Every word, however, when we have the intent to bind and *loose* is binding or *loosing* something. Every act and every action are binding or *loosing* **something**. All day and all night. because we are either blocking or allowing something to come into our life all day long.

What we see in the natural, sure, but in the spirit, there is something being allowed or blocked by our words, deeds, actions--, by our choices. Something real and perhaps eternal is happening in the spirit by what we are doing in the natural, all the time. As well, what is already in the spirit realm affects what we think and do and how life impacts us and how we impact lives here in the Earth realm. Perhaps this is why the Word says we are to walk circumspectly, and to be wise.

Sin is thinking to do a thing that is evil. The transgression is actually doing it. We are binding or *loosing*, allowing or disallowing a thing in our own lives or the lives of others--- our family or bloodline even by our thoughts. Else, why would God be judging the thoughts and intentions of the heart? Evil thoughts and plans are the beginning of evil acts, and they are sin.

For the word of God is quick, and powerful, and sharper than any twoedged sword, piercing even to the dividing asunder of soul and spirit, and of the joints and marrow, and is a discerner of the thoughts and intents of the heart. (Hebrews 4:12)

You, yourself, you do not like evil hearted people. A person with an evil heart may never do anything evil in their whole life, but there is something about them that you just don't like. Well, even if this person never transgresses, he (or she) is inviting or allowing whatever that evil is into his bloodline. There comes a second generation. There will come a third generation. The first man's evil heart has invited or allowed this evil into the bloodline. Have you ever met a baby that is just not kind or friendly, like from birth? Why is anyone born a certain way? It is spiritual and it is based on what is in that foundation.

Where did a person's *foundation* come from? His parents or ancestors. Whatever he is born into, conceived in sin and created in iniquity, the baby's job is to act out what has been prescribed for him (or her), by their parents and other ancestors who created their spiritual foundation.

Behold, I was shapen in iniquity; and in sin did my mother conceive me. (Psalm 51:5)

The only way to overcome foundational programming is in Christ, by Christ Jesus. Amen.

Sinning for Others

When I see someone with extra short fingernails, sometimes being silly, I will ask the person, *"Do you bite your own nails, or do you have someone to come in and do it for you?"* They usually laugh and that awareness makes them realize that it is a habit that they really want to stop. Then I say something about the teeth--, how nails can wear the teeth needlessly. Then I talk about the germs that they carry to their mouth when putting their dirty hands in their mouth so often in a day. Yes, I have asked people if they wash their hands before they start biting their teeth. They glare at me. I hold their glare. You wash your hands before dinner, right?

None of these statements are to embarrass them but give them things to think about and remember the next time their hands come up to their mouth. It has often worked.

So silly--, I know that others do not bite people's nails for them, but others can **sin** for you. And, you can sin for others, whether you realize it or not. I ask again— are you your brother's keeper? I ask it often because I am guilty for years of thinking that I was not my brother's keeper. But, yes we are, especially when it comes to **bloodline sin**, bloodline iniquity, and bloodline open spiritual doors. The person of highest spiritual authority in a family can do the most good and also the most harm in a family and for a family. That doesn't mean others of lower position or less authority can't do good or evil. It's just that more authority wields more power.

Wisdom *is* better than weapons of war: but one sinner destroyeth much good.
(Ecclesiastes 9:18)

But when sin and the consequences of sin are upon a person, did they sin or did someone else? That is addressed in the New Testament.

> And his disciples asked him, saying, Master, who did sin, this man or his parents, that he was born blind? (John 9:2)

Obviously, that is a real thing to sin *prophetically--*, to sin into one's generations, to sin so that the **iniquity** passes into the generations and into one's future.

Remember, when you sin, you don't just sin for yourself, you sin for others too – especially your children and your *children's* children, whether or not they are yet born. God is coming to *visit* to the third and the fourth generation and in that *visit* God is seeing how you did because if your children don't know God that is accounted against you.

> Thou shalt not bow down thyself to them, nor serve them: for I the LORD thy God *am* a jealous God, visiting the iniquity of the fathers upon the children unto the third and fourth *generation* of them that hate me (Exodus 20:5)

In that *visit*, if they know and obey God, then hallelujah, that is accounted to you.

Children, the fruit of your womb, the fruit of your loins that continue to serve GOD is another definition of fruit that remains. *Children are fruit.* It's why they say, "The fruit don't fall far from the tree;" it's because children are fruit. They should be fruit that remains in Christ. Fruit that remains faithful. Fruit that remains productive. Much fruit, and fruit that remains. Hallelujah and Amen.

So, wouldn't it be logical that you make it as doable, as smooth, as easy as possible for your children and your children's children to remain in Christ? Yes, for their sakes but God is also coming at the third and fourth generation *visit*, and **you will be judged by the spiritual condition of your kids** because that will reflect back on you. Depending on what your kids and your grandkids look like spiritually will inform the Lord as to your own faithfulness to Him.

You make that possible by teaching your children at all times, making sure they know the Word of God, not by beating it into them, but by priesting, by representing Christ in the family.

How can you do that? By binding and *loosing*. By allowing or disallowing things into the bloodline. You would not put up or leave a known obstacle in your family's life, would you? You would tear down evil interferences that propose to place themselves in your bloodline that do not align with the will and purpose of God, right? You've got keys. You've got authority. You've got power in Christ, expressly for the purpose of clearing the path that your children and their children must pass to be successful in life.

Abraham tithed in Levi. That was 3 generations into Abraham's future; Levi was his great grandson.

And as I may so say, Levi also, who receiveth tithes, payed tithes in Abraham.
(Hebrews 7:9)

By binding and *loosing* you are either allowing or disallowing spiritual things into your bloodline. By knowing what tithing accomplishes or does spiritually and naturally, by tithing in Levi, Abraham disallowed scarcity, lack, insufficiency, poverty in Levi. He allowed God, prosperity and abundance.

Call It What It Is

In the Book of Genesis. God let Adam name everything, and whatever Adam called it, that is what it was named.

Whatever the man called every living creature became its name. (Genesis 2:19)

As the patriarch of your family, as the matriarch, intercessor, called one, chosen one, prophet, priest, apostle, evangelist – whatever you are in your family –whatever God has called you or whatever position He has put you in, you have spiritual responsibility to that calling and position. Perhaps you are the Phinehas of your family or generation. It doesn't make you better than them, it doesn't mean you should get a big ring and spout off Scriptures to them. It means you have spiritual work to do and most of it may be in private in your prayer closet with just you and God there. It is standing in the gap for those you have charge over or those you pray for.

Phinehas, the son of Eleazar, the son of Aaron the priest, hath turned my wrath away from the children of Israel, while he was zealous for my sake among them, that I consumed not the children of Israel in my jealousy.

Wherefore say, Behold, I give unto him my covenant of peace:

And he shall have it, and his seed after him, even the covenant of an everlasting priesthood; because he was zealous for his God, and made an atonement for the children of Israel. (Numbers 25:11-13)

Phinehas is not the only one who made intercession for others. Abraham did it (somewhat) for Lot. Moses did it so the multitude could enter the Promised Land, even though he, himself didn't get in. Jesus did it and does it for all of us; He is Our Great Intercessor, and you as an elder, watchman, intercessor, or priest of your house or family should be doing that as well for your house.

You have authority to bind and *loose*. To block or allow. To allow or disallow. In so doing, you also are naming. *How so?* When something evil comes upon you or your family, you **name** it as **evil**, identify it and disallow it or block it.

You've got keys; you've got authority.

You are naming good things, as blessings, calling them what they are -- blessings from God and you are allowing them – right? Amen. You are naming things, similar to Adam. And, you are also discerning things, determining good from bad, calling them what they are, naming them and governing yourself, accordingly.

Woe to those who call evil good and good evil. If you misname a thing, you may keep it around when you should be dismissing it or getting rid of it. When you misname a good thing, you may mistakenly get rid of it when you should keep it.

Woe to those who call evil good and good evil, who turn darkness to light and light to darkness, who replace bitter with sweet and sweet with bitter. (Isaiah 5:20)

So, in this authority, with the keys, you must also use discernment. Discernment is a gift from God, and it is sharpened by use. Therefore, with this keen discernment, you rightly judge and rightly divide good from evil. You rightly accept or reject this as important.

You are allowing or disallowing by your accepting or rejecting, that is binding and *loosing*. Not just for yourself but also for your family and your bloodline. It is not always immediate, iniquity takes time, sometimes. It is not always quick; your kids may not have been born yet, but you are:

- Looking at and dealing with the foundation that you've been dealt based on the family you were born into.
- Or not. You may be doing absolutely nothing, so the foundation you got is the same one your kids will get.

- And you are preparing foundation for your children based on your holiness or sins, and repentance or lack thereof.

This is especially important if you are in a high position in your bloodline, either because God called you to be there, or you are perhaps left as the eldest in your family, how you remain in the bloodline while others may have predeceased you. Yes, mourn, but you can't stay in mourning because you have work to do, perhaps even more work now that your family elders are gone and you are now the eldest, or the called one by God for your family.

And, once you marry and have kids, you are the parent, the one with the most authority in that branch of your bloodline.

In your authority, you rightly divide good from evil; you accept or reject things. Let's say your kid brings home a puppy they found. The puppy doesn't just affect your kid, it affects the whole house. When the door was opened for the puppy, everything changed. Now that change may not be generational, but I use that example to show whatever is let into the family, or the house affects everyone.

But strong meat belongeth to them that are of full age, even those who by reason of use have their senses exercised to discern both good and evil. (Hebrews 5:14)

Whatever you bind or *loose* in Earth is also bound or loosed in Heaven Allowing or disallowing by accepting and rejecting. This does not mean that others in the family do not have their own free will, but as the authority you are setting the tone. This is very much like the leader of anything, even a country accepts or rejects things from the top. When the leader starts *acting a monkey*, the rest of the country may go into mayhem. If the leader is ordered and has self-control, you will find the majority will behave in a like manner. The same is true for a family.

It Is Written

Things are written down in the Heavenlies. God is a careful bookkeeper; else, how could He be a Righteous Judge without evidence and records? Writing things down was so important to God that He, by His own Hand wrote the first tablets of the Ten Commandments. This is critical in things of the spirit realm, that things be written down. So, when Moses came down from the mountain and saw the rampant idolatry, he became angry, broke the tablets and then he had to go back on the mountain to have God speak those Commandments to him again. Then Moses wrote the second tablets because the Commandments had to be written down.

In those Ten Commandments, the first set God wrote with His own finger, God was writing what He allows and what He disallows. He wrote what He accepts and what He rejects. That's the type of family meeting a priest of a home, for example, could have with his family.

Office policy and manuals are **written down**. Anything in the Law is usually written down. It outlines what is acceptable and what is not.

Jim Bob disallowed poverty in his life and the life of his family by his actions. This may be what is heard or sounded in the Heavenlies. The next thing you may hear is, "Write that down." (Actually, it is automatically recorded, God doesn't need to micromanage angels.) Those who serve willingly and respectfully do not need to be micromanaged, in Heaven or Earth. And that is called Grace.

So, most likely, it was already written when Jim Bob **thought** it or decided it --, even before he even spoke it. That is a decree or a fiat, an ordinance, perhaps a law. Why? Because by virtue of being a man born in the Earth, Jim Bob has a certain authority. Jim Bob has keys. Jim Bob, by receiving

Salvation by Christ Jesus and by faith has disallowed poverty in his life and in the life of his family. Jim Bob did that by his acts in the Earth; he got a good career, kept his job or business, and paid his bills. Jim Bob disallowed poverty in his life and established that for his family. It was written in his foundation.

Marianne disallowed sickness in herself, her family and her bloodline. She allowed divine health in her life and in her bloodline; "– Write that down. Write that down may be heard in the heavenlies. She did it by staying in the Word of God and claiming the promises of Salvation in Christ for herself. It may have been just for herself, but it could have been for a family member, her child—but it could have been just for herself. AND in so doing, because she as a woman standing in authority perhaps interceding or priesting in her God given role, in her family, and in so doing now her children and generations reap the same established for their lives. They may still have to ask for it and claim it, but it is there for them because of Marianne and her position of authority.

In the spirit the question may be heard, *Did you write that down?* Now it is recorded in the heavens, and the notation is made in the spiritual foundation.

When your kids watch you allow or disallow, yes that is modeling in the natural, but things are being recorded in the spirit realm that you will or will not allow certain things in your life and by extension, in your family's life and in your bloodline. Your children grow up expecting to have a nice house, a spouse, a good career, a family. Else, why would so many members of the same family look the same as it pertains to the things that are related to their lives and godliness? It is spiritual. And by allowing you are *naming* a thing as good, okay, I want that, I'll keep that. Or the counter.

Sometimes in a family, for example, one or more in that family may supersede what is "allowed" spiritually. That is when and why struggles confront those achievers in that bloodline. These limitations created or prescribed must be overcome spiritually. They can only be overcome in Christ.

By Christ – In Christ

Jesus answered, "I am the way and the truth and the life. No one comes to the Father except through me. (John 14:6)

Were it not for Jesus' work, His crucifixion and death, and Him taking on the sins of the world and then God resurrecting Him, we could not be saved. It is by Grace that we are saved. We are saved by faith in God, and this is a gift of God. However, if we do not receive Jesus for ourselves, we are not saved. We are not saved because mom, dad, grandma or grandpa are saved. Sadly, sin can be generational, but salvation is not. Salvation is an individual decision and requires a personal walk with the Lord.

If you declare with your mouth, "Jesus is Lord," and believe in your heart that God raised him from the dead, you will be saved. (Romans 10:9)

Your parent could be the pastor of a church, it doesn't make you saved, anymore than a man who has an uncle who is a professor at MIT make that man smart.

There was a woman whose husband became a General in the Airforce, off base she believed she had certain entitlements as if she also was a General. It doesn't work like that.

Jesus died for us all, but we must receive Him personally for ourselves. Reading the Bible, listening to teachers and ministry lessons doesn't make a person saved. Being a kind or good person doesn't make a person saved. Having guilt after sin, well at least you still have a conscience, but that doesn't make you saved.

Only by Christ are you or any of us saved.

Only in Christ can you make these binding and *loosing* declarations and decrees with the proper authority that makes the spirit realm pay attention. All else? You're just talking.

Unfortunately, the things you say and do on the dark side will be seen, captured, recorded, done. Without being in Christ a person is easily caught, tricked, initiated, covenanted and they may know nothing about it. They could be shown anything and everything in a dream and that dream could be wiped, so they remain in the dark. This is why it is too dangerous not to remember your dreams.

In Christ means you are fully in, not hanging around the edge of Christianity. You know, like Christianity is a buffet and you can pick and choose the parts that you like. Some like to choose what they see as the fun parts, the music, the dancing, cool gear to wear--, the seen parts.

Everything they do is for show. On their arms they wear extra wide prayer boxes with Scripture verses inside, and they wear robes with extra long tassels. (Matthew 23:5)

What about the real and silent parts, the unseen parts of the Faith? What about the daily praying? The fasting? The consecration? The repentance, the intercession and praying for others? What about agreeing with your adversary quickly when you may want to move in pride and show them a thing or two? What about self-righteousness? What about secret and hidden sin? Will you stop it, or believe that if people don't know, then God doesn't know?

What about dying to the flesh? Will you forgive? Will you be delivered from covetousness and jealousy? What about praise and worship? What about giving and sacrifice? What about discernment? A Christian walk is 24/7; that is what it means to be in Christ—communing with God, actually, hearing God, and obeying God.

Now, that you're fully **in**, you may bind and *loose* and you may implore the agency, treasury, and give voice to the Word of God and expect results in your favor.

Anything less? Your words will be considered idle, or lip service.

But thou, when thou prayest, enter into thy closet, and when thou hast shut thy door, pray to thy Father which is in secret; and thy Father which seeth in secret shall reward thee openly. (Matthew 6:6)

Prescribed

These allowed or disallowed things are recorded in heavenly places, and they are codified to keep spiritual matters – that actually <u>create</u> physical conditions from being other than what YOU, yes, Y.O.U. **prescribed**. By what you allow or disallow you are prescribing for your life, for your children, for your family, for your business, for your future. You are **naming**. You are calling. You are decreeing and declaring what you agree with, what you want, because you have authority by being set in authority.

You have keys. You have authority, you have power when you have keys. That power binds things to you or it *looses* things and they are then to leave or be cast away from you, your family, and your bloodline.

Angels obey the voice of the Word of God. Marianne claimed the promises of Salvation found in the Word of God, she believed, she received, she spoke them – they were already written in the Word of God and now they are written in the Spirit that this woman, Marianne has accepted the Word and the Will of God. In so doing, she has rejected anything and everything that is not the Word or the Will of God. Let it be written and this is what must be done because it is the Word of God that she has given voice to. It is the voice of the Word of God, and this is what angels obey. Furthermore, this decision is recorded.

Saints of God do you see your authority here? You may think that only kings have scribes, but what you say, do, even think is recorded. Good or bad; it is recorded. Yes, in the heavenlies – the devil on the evil side is trying to entrap humans, while God is recording for other reasons. FYI, Jesus is the King of kings – we are all little k kings in the Earth.

Angels obey the Word of God by causing it to come to pass, causing it to happen, and because of your covenant of Salvation with God there are things that cannot be allowed to happen to you or against you. Certain things are precluded from happening to you because of your covenant in Christ. Because you bound and *loosed*, you spoke, you allowed or disallowed, you accepted or rejected using the Word of God and therefore it was written, and it was written of you.

It is written **first**. In Psalm 40, Jesus said, **"I come in the volume of the book where it is written of Me."** It was written <u>first</u>, then it is done. It is written in the spirit realm first, then it is done. It was already written in the spirit and then it was fulfilled – that is prophecy. It was already written before Jesus got here. It was written first and then it is done. It is written in the spirit realm first and then it is done in the Earth realm.

Notwithstanding in this rejoice not, that the spirits are subject unto you; but rather rejoice, because your names are written in heaven. (Luke 10:20)

Whatever you bind in Earth is also bound in heaven. What you *loose* on Earth is loosed in heaven.

Prescribed means it is prewritten, that is why you sometimes see the horrible or mischievous kids of good people seeming to get away with things that they shouldn't be getting away with. Because Marianne or Grandma or someone *prescribed* for good things for the bloodline. It could be that the ancestors and parents walked upright before God and are under Grace while a rebellious member of the family's iniquity hasn't caught up with the perpetrator yet.

Frank does not agree that home insecurity should be in his life, family or bloodline. Devils, demons and evil human agents be put on notice that Frank does not allow that. When Frank believed it and said it, then it was written on Heavenly scrolls, tablets or slates.

But let's say the enemy tries to take Bill's house and Bill is unaware, not discerning, distracted, doesn't care, is sinning, so there is a *cause* for this judgment to alight. Bill is not properly priesting over his own life or over his family's life, so he does nothing; he is just goofing off. You cannot do godly priesting and sin at the same time.

Unfortunately, perhaps the enemy is successful at taking Bill's house because Bill is an unrepentant sinner. The Lord will hear our prayers of repentance, but Bill isn't repenting. But bill got angry, quit his job and stopped paying his mortgage. That's a real obvious way not to live in your own house.

Or maybe just as obvious, Bill got caught up in sexual sin with a side chick, and his wife divorced him and took the house, or it had to be sold as per terms of the divorce.

Even less obvious, Bill agreed in some evil covenant that he would just give up his house in exchange for whatever he wanted from the devil. Maybe Bill was looking for a shortcut and got into something occultic and was looking for the easy way out of his situation. The terms of that evil covenant is also recorded, although Bill may not even know what he agreed to, or that he agreed to anything. Bill may only be thinking about what he is getting—that desired something. But these are all temptations, Bill thinks he has turned a stone into bread and even while he is falling and the devil can't send any angels to catch him, he is thinking about the kingdoms of the world that he has been promised and thinks he is getting.

Bill's binding and *loosing* is all recorded--, not just for Bill, for now, for his life, it is recorded for up to three or four of Bill's generations. If those kids hate God, then the contract and evil covenant is extended. Then devils and demons may have legal rights to Bill's house, and Bill's kids' and grandkids' houses and so on for three to four generations. This could explain why in some families owning or house or having house security is such a struggle or commonly impossible.

Bill opened the door. Bill let it in. Bill let it stay and dwell in his house. Bill didn't repent. Priest of the house, Bill, improperly priesting, set in spiritual authority sinned for the whole family, the family to come and the family after that. Dad Bill, Grandpa Bill and Great-Grandpa Bill, the great unrepentant sinner of the bloodline. Bill set the spiritual situation for himself, his family and his bloodline.

You have the **keys**. Do you just want to know you have them yet just let them jiggle in your pocket, or will you do something with them?

Your binding and *loosing writes* things in the spirit realm.

Scribes

My heart is indicting a good matter: I speak
of the things which I have made touching
the king: my tongue *is* the pen of a ready
writer. (Psalm 45:1)

Scribes are the writers who record
very important things, and usually for
posterity. Who had Scribes back in Bible
times? Important people, kings and
governmental authorities, religious figures.
Scribes responsible for writing and copying
texts, often serving important roles in
religious and administrative contexts.

Scribes copied sacred texts, including
the Torah, and ensured the accurate
transmission of religious laws and teachings.

They recorded legal documents, census data, and other official records for governments and institutions.

In ancient Egypt, scribes held high status and were trained in writing and managing state affairs. The greatest civilizations, empires or dynasties were great because they wrote things down. Roman Scribes of the Roman Empire worked for government officials. Ezra was a scribe who worked in the return of the Jewish exiles and re-establishing the Law in Jerusalem (Ezra 7:6).

Jeremiah employed a scribe named Baruch to write down his prophecies (Jeremiah 36:4). King Jehoikaim did not like the prophecies of Jeremiah that Baruch, Jeremiah's scribe had recorded. Jehoikaim burned the scrolls. God was not pleased. So Jeremiah had to dictate the prophecy all over again so it could be recorded. God requires things to be written down. Scribes are critical in preserving and disseminating knowledge particularly biblical and historical records. As a scribe, writing things implies writing them down.

We hear words spoken and often forget them, and we may think those words went away, vanished into thin air. They did not. They remain. Your words are the fruit of your lips. You should always bear good fruit, because it will remain. Just realizing that everything you do, say, even think is written down should sober all of us up, spiritually speaking.

Writing things in the spirit as with the pen of a ready writer means praying, saying, decreeing and declaring. I'd call that writing things up rather than writing them down.

All interfaces with the spiritual realm are through altars, so it depends on your personal, family, bloodline, church, corporate, national altar as to who can hear what you are saying and who considers it worthwhile to write down. As well, what backing do you have for what you are saying to make spiritual entities obey? That means will they help you, if they are on God's side? Will they leave you alone if they are on the dark side? This is what happens in the background of binding and *loosing*.

Now, God transcends all time and space. Prayers transcend time and space. As a prophet of God, a prayer warrior, intercessor, who is well connected through Jesus Christ, what you say carries weight. Unsaved people can speak and what they say is also recorded, but saved people, saints of God, what we say is more weighty and **more** powerful.

> But I say unto you, That every idle word
> that men shall speak, they shall give
> account thereof in the day of judgment.
> (Matthew 12:36)

Those idle words you have to give account of? They are written in the spirit. There are thrones in Heaven where God holds Court – there are transcripts in courts.

So, to *pre*-scribe a thing is an authority given to man by God. As God is visiting to the third and fourth generation, it's like saying I'll be back in a few generations and will see how you are doing. I've given you My Word and everything you need for life and godliness, I will see you (your bloodline) in a few generations. But that doesn't mean that no one is looking while

47

God is not "visiting." Further, it would be better if the presence of God was there the whole time to guide you by His Spirit so you can avoid trouble.

But the authority to speak, like God, into generations is a mercy God affords man by what that man says stands as he is pre-scribing what is allowed or disallowed in his own life, his family, or his bloodline. So as men we must use the authority and power to better our own lives, the lives of our bloodline that we were born into and especially our direct bloodline, our children and our children's children.

It's like having a certain limit on your credit card where you don't have to call in for authorization if it is under that established "floor limit." How is this possible? The things you speak over people either come to pass or if you are saying they will not do such and such or accomplish things, those things don't come to pass. That is pre-scribing. It has been written in the heavenlies prior to the time that it should or should not happen. It doesn't make you right necessarily, it might not even make you smart or kind, but it meant that you had or were given authority to speak over that person's life.

Saying evil things like the following is also prescribing. When evil is spoken, it is the words of witches and blind witches:

- That boy will never amount to anything.
- That person is not smart, and they will barely finish high school.
- That child cannot cook; they will not keep a spouse.
- She's this that or other – no one will want to marry her.

Why would you want to pre-write or prescribe such a thing for a person to either never overcome or completely succumb to it? Those are evil imaginations and they are witchcraft. And, especially why would ou want to prescribe such a thing for a relative or family member? Why would you want to curse them? Carefully consider your binding and *loosing* whether you are using words or taking actions so you don't curse your own children.

Saints of God, what is bound or loosed is recorded in Heaven first. Let's look at this verse again.

I will give you the keys of the kingdom of heaven; and whatever you bind on earth shall have been bound in heaven, and whatever you loose on earth shall have been loosed in heaven. (Matthew 16:19)

Whatever you bind on Earth, **shall have been** bound in heaven. Shall have been means that it already happened in the spirit realm and not it comes into the Earth realm. So, when you have a vision or a night vision (dream) and you see a thing that thing is or has happened in the spirit realm already. If you want it to come to Earth then pray that way. If you want to stop it, block it or disallow it from coming into the Earth realm then pray that way. Be expedient with your prayers. Right away is the best time. I heard it said that there is a 72 hour delay in seeing it in the dream and it manifesting in the Earth. Either way, handle it. There is no promise that something good will just come to you because you saw it in a dream.

Why not?

Because the devil wants to block you from getting that blessing, and most likely he wants to steal it and have it for himself to use to tempt some other unsuspecting person.

You have **keys**: Binding and *loosing*.

For best results if you want to pray a blessing through, open up a case in the Courts of Heaven. If you want to block some evil that you've seen in your dream from manifesting in the Earth realm—open up a case in the Courts of Heaven.

Take action. If you want it to come to Earth, then act like it, be like it—believe it—that is faith. If you don't want it to come into the Earth realm, then you have to believe, as touching, that it is precluded and shall not be. Faith with works is what makes Faith alive.

Allowing - Disallowing

When you <u>allow</u> something it gets a foothold into your family. Especially if you are the priest of that house. The matriarch, the patriarch, the intercessor, watchman— whatever position God has called you to, what you let in can be disastrous for your family even over time and generations. Especially if you are the highest authority of that bloodline. if it is sin, IT IS WRITTEN. and If you do not repent then it stays there-- written.

Repentance is a form of binding and *loosing*. It is binding the enemy from doing anything further to you and they are loosed, that is, dislodged from your family/bloodline/foundation. Repentance is for the purpose of removing the judgment and erasing the iniquity and the cause that allowed evil to alight into a life or household.

If you <u>didn't</u> sin, but you realize there are some ungodly spiritual things happening in your family – it got there by cause. 'Cause somebody in your ancestry allowed it, hid it, tried to hide it, pretended it didn't happen, and then did nothing about it.

But they had keys and did nothing with the keys. They had keys but may not have known they had keys. They may have had too much pride to use the keys, the right way, humbling themselves under the Mighty Hand of God.

They had the keys: the authority, they had power, the ability, but did the wrong things with that power, with the keys. Perhaps they lorded over everyone in the house, declaring him or herself as king or queen and decided they could do anything they wanted--, including sin.

Not so.

If you realize that has happened in your bloodline and you also do nothing about it, then you too are saying you agree. In that agreement you are allowing it. In allowing it, you are agreeing. If two or three agree, it shall be done. Sometimes you agree by not disagreeing. In the mouth of two or three witnesses, let every word be established.

In the mouth
of two or three witnesses shall every word
be established (2 Corinthians 13:1-4)

So, if your ancestor sinned and did nothing about it, or you think what you or your ancestor did was cool or fun or funny, then you are simply agreeing with that sin. That agreement either lets demons in to oppress and enforce, or it keeps them in your bloodline, giving the demons a stronger position, perhaps from foothold to stronghold to oppression or possession.

Repent. Repent down your bloodline else it stands all the more. You have keys.

How did you agree – again by doing nothing. If you say things like:

- I can't do anything about it.
- *That's just the way our family is.*

- That's just what happens to us.
- All the people in my family ---- went by this way or had this or lost that.

You are agreeing with the evil that is already there. So, don't say that. Instead say and do what God says because you have keys. in Christ you have keys to get into any Godly thing that God allows you to get into. In Christ you have the keys to get out of anything ungodly.

Will it be easy? Not saying it will be quick or easy, it depends on your faith, it depends on how long it's been there, it depends on your walk with the Lord. But by your prayers, decrees and declarations you are saying, as for me and my house we will serve the Lord.

As for me and my house:

- I ALLOW <u>THIS</u> IN MY FAMILY.
- I *DISALLOW* <u>THIS</u> IN MY FAMILY.

You are speaking to spiritual realms to make them take notice. First the angels of God will **cause** Godly things that you allow to happen to you and your bloodline. And you are speaking to the dark side saying this is a no-fly zone, do not come in here or around here because we don't allow that in our bloodline. Make sure the dark side knows ungodly things are not allowed. You do all this with the **keys**. I do not allow that evil in my family.

Make sure that you are allowing or disallowing in the authority of Christ--, in the Name of Jesus, not just your own authority.

You are saying: I allow these blessings. I receive these blessings from the Lord. And I will do what is required of me to walk upright before the Lord to receive these blessings from the Lord.

Timewise, saints of God, I pray that the deliverance and the change and the breakthrough and the restoration will be quick and expedient, but even if it is not— the binding and *loosing* has started. Now your children and their children have a different foundation because you allowed GOD or invited Him, and you disallowed and disinvited the enemy. If it starts with you, then let it start with you, Amen. Then bring the entire family along, in the Lord. Amen.

You allowed abundance and disallowed poverty.

You allowed house, land, and property ownership and rejected loss and disappointment and housing insecurity, in your life, in your family, in your bloodline, in the Name of Jesus.

You allow or disallow by your thoughts, words, deeds, and actions, or your inaction.

In the Next Generation

If you allow something in the natural – remember there is a spiritual counterpart to it – so now, in the next generation it will be worse. If you allow it, it's a foothold. Next generation it is a stronghold. Next generation it is even worse, oppression or possession, for example. So, by the time God *visits* the third generation on your great grandfather – because **that is you**, pray for Mercy. Pray for Mercy, in the Name of Jesus.

Remember the kid who found the puppy and brought it home? Now that puppy is of age and has a litter of puppies. You had one puppy that turned into a dog and now there are 7 puppies in your house. That is what the next generation looks like. These spirits act on the buddy model—if one gets in they will invite their evil buddies, or as the Word says go and get seven more worse than itself and come back. It will be quite an infestation.

> Then it goes and takes with it seven other spirits more wicked than itself, and they go in and live there. And the final condition of that person is worse than the first. That is how it will be with this wicked generation.
> (Matthew 12:45 NIV)

A puppy is not sin, but I used that for example. So, if sin is allowed in the 1st generation, unrepented sin no matter how it has been hidden, slipped under the rug, or ignored, in the second generation its worse, way worse. People try to mask sin with other sins if they are not repenting. They say in the natural that the coverup is worse than the crime. Same goes in spiritual matters.

For example: 1ST generation divination turns into idolatry by the second generation. By the third it shows up as barrenness, poverty, slavery. Where you work, work, work and it doesn't even look like you have a job. First generation sin and iniquity gets into the second generation because it is not repented of. A woman gave testimony that her child cannot have children. Of course, all things are possible with God, but is that not a work of barrenness? Barrenness is a sequela of divination at least two generations ago.

The Hebrews were in Egypt, the kingdom of idol gods; they had a god for everything and worshipped pretty much everything. They were no strangers to divination. The Hebrews were there 430 years. Do you think they had occasion to bump into a diviner from time to time? Now they cry out to God who sets them free and they just got across the Red Sea and are in the Wilderness. Moses goes up to meet with God and get the Ten Commandments and these newly freed slaves are doing what? Making a golden calf to worship. Idolatry.

Generational sin invites devils, demons and unclean *spirits* in and it gets worse from generation to generation.

1st generation fornication will show up in the 2nd generation as impurity, which is defilement and uncleanness. This can also lead to blindness, rejection, or demonic possession when it gets embedded in the bloodline by the third generation. Is this spiritual blindness or blindness in the natural – pray; it could be ether or both.

In the New Testament, the Disciples asked Jesus when they encountered a blind man who needed to be healed, "Who sinned, this man or his parents?"

Jesus answered, it is for the Glory of God. This is telling us that when God heals a person and they are made whole, God is not just healing symptoms. God is going back into the generations and forgiving sin and erasing iniquity from a foundation, and He is doing it in Time because Time is subject to God. When the sin is forgiven and the iniquity is removed, the stickiness of the curse is removed and the symptoms must go.

You may be thinking that it would be handy to know what leads to what, but you don't want any of it. You don't want any of it to dwell in your house because that resident sin will destroy a house completely. Surely, you are not willing to sin for your generations that come after you, knowing that their lives will be worse than yours? Their lives may be totally wasted. You do care what happens to them, *right*? If you do not care, then you need to get saved and fully converted.

There was a woman who would often steal from her siblings. She'd simply go to their house and take what she wanted. If left there alone, or if no one was looking she'd go on a stealing spree. When confronted with theft, she would then "confess" that she didn't think her siblings would mind once they saw how much she wanted the item she took, or how happy it would make her to have it.

Of course that is not confession, but that is how selfish sinners and criminals think. Me, me, me. Now, now, now. They learned it from the devil. She needs to get saved and fully converted.

We all think that new babies are born with a clean slate – no, that slate has been scarred, marred, marked up, evil ordinances have been written on that slate or pinned to it. Evil marks, evil covenants – that cute, sweet, innocent looking baby may have inherited iniquity and unrepented sin and has all that against them already. Prescriptions have been written on that baby's slate and life. You may have been that baby and life has been coming at you from out of no where. You know you didn't do anything to deserve the troubles you've had up to this point. Because if you knew, you could have repented, right?

No matter how much you love your child, no matter how much you wish the best for them, you have to deal with what has been written in the spirit already against this family, against this bloodline, against that innocent baby, or it will remain and could get worse. This baby is the next generation, after all.

The Word says to train up a child… we train children more by who we are than by who we think we are or who we want to be, or who we want them to be. When they are old, they shall not depart from it. They can't depart from the foundation that they've inherited, except in Christ.

YOU HAVE THE KEYS.

Unless you've used the keys that have been given to you by Jesus Christ what is written will remain written, and be enforced and could get even worse

The foundation sets the pattern. Anyone who sews, makes things or even builds things knows that if the measurement is wrong the part you cut won't fit. If you keep using the faulty pattern to measure and or trace or cut, the next generation of what you are making will be far worse than the original.

Without Works

We are not just binding and *loosing* without also doing works because without faith it is impossible to please God (Hebrews 11:6) and faith without works is dead (James 2:26). Works prove that you have faith, else you wouldn't act. So now you have to put yourself into action to carry out the decrees and declarations of what you believe in your life. Yes, so your family can see you and you can be a role model. And it is so you and they can both benefit and be encouraged by it, but also you are making a spiritual mark on that slate of your family. It is a Godly mark, a Godly statement of what you will allow or disallow.

You are writing spiritually speaking about you, yourself, but it you are in a position of authority in your family you are allowing a certain grace and disallowing disgraces over your family about your bloodline.

Everything allowed gets at least a foot in the door or a wide-open door to come into your bloodline at will over at least three to four generations. Hey, that's the time frame, unless someone stops it. Hopefully someone in your bloodline who notices it and closes the open doors, spiritually. Some one that God has called and authorized, either by calling or by spiritual title. A watchman in the gap, a prophet, an intercessor, a prayer warrior, a mom or a dad, grandma, grandpa, a Phinehas in your family line--, someone with spiritual Wisdom and authority.

In the same way it could be noticed that good doors, good gates, good opportunities may not be coming to your family and someone in authority and position has to invite those blessings, ask the Lord and invoke those blessings – God's way, no other way. Blessings are coming up to overtake, therefore this bloodline has to have the Grace to receive those blessings.

Are you kidding? Some people cannot even receive a compliment, it takes Grace. Pray and ask the Lord for Grace to receive blessings. Amen.

In your binding and *loosing*, using those spiritual keys, you are declaring:

- We are about this.
- We are about God.
- We allow this.
- We don't allow that.
- We bind this.
- We *loose* that.
- We accept this.
- We don't accept that.
- We receive this.
- We reject that, all in the Name of Jesus. Amen.

This is all done a certain way – we don't malign and beat others across the head to make them. Not by power or by might, but by the Spirit of the Lord let these things be done in your life, family and bloodline. Amen.

Patience Versus Complacency

If devils, demons, or unclean *spirits* know that you don't really stand for anything, or that you think that neutral is a spiritual choice, when it is not, then it's open season and anything goes. They'll do anything to you that they can. Many people think that if you don't bother the devil he won't bother you. that doesn't work with people, so how would it work with the devil? The devil is who inspires people to irk you, bother you, hate you, compete with you for no reason at all. People you've done nothing to, haven't bothered, and may have only been kind and gracious to--, even in your own family may just feel some kinda way about you or have animosity to you. Even from childhood there may have been bullies or later in life, haters. That's all devil work, in people you've done nothing to. So that theory doesn't stand. If you have an iota of anointing, goodness, purpose or destiny in you, you will be bothered no matter how kind you are to folks. In the natural if you look nice, have nice things, aren't starving or if you look successful, there will be people who will bother you, no matter how kind you are to them. A people pleaser is the one who thinks, Hey, I was nice and they still did that to me, so now I'll just be nicer.

Don't do that. You will give yourself away.

If the enemy thinks a person will work the spiritual gift of Patience all the way into complacency without getting up to do any works, then they will run all over such a person. Don't wait until way late in life to realize that you didn't know the timing of God, that is, when to wait, when to rest in Him, and when to work.

The kingdom of Heaven suffers violence.

Faith without works is dead.

Those who habitually do little or nothing, while constantly going through, and suffering saying, *"I'm just waiting on the Lord,"* are the types to do nothing while suffering or living in defeat, needlessly. Your doing nothing when you should be binding or *loosing*, or doing something, signals the spirit realm that you are okay with what the devil is dishing out.

Saints, the fact that there is a bully, or hater in the natural means whatever is happening in your life already happened in the spirit realm and either nothing was done to stop it or nothing was either done to try to stop it, or it is God's judgment and it couldn't be stopped --- except for Mercy. Did you at least cry to God for Mercy?

The Lord's Will be done. (Look in the Bible, then you will know the Lord's Will. Get up and do that. Amen.

One day my change will come. (Really?)

The man at the pool of Bethesda was there for 38 years. Seasons changed, years changed, but his condition did not for all that time. Jesus told that man to get up and take up his bed. Does Jesus need to say that to you? He can, you know, because it is in His Will. A Testament is a Will. **Get up and walk is in the LORD's Will.**

Why are babies determined even from birth to get up? Why are babies determined to get up and walk? To escape from the captivity of cribs? To run? Because we are programmed to obey God. Get up and walk.

What happens to us after that? Seek God in your particular case but my guess is like in the Garden of Eden, as soon as we are born the devil begins to reverse, pervert, or remove God's divine programming in us. And, he does it through situations, circumstances, conditions, our foundation and people.

Well meaning but exasperated parents may be guilty of this. Those who do not parent God's way. Parents who have a bad foundation themselves cannot pass on anything other than what they have. Not what they had, what they have, we can all be made new creatures in Christ. Our foundations can be healed--, in Christ.

Stating what God said about you is Godly, it is binding and *loosing*, it is warfare. Saints of God it is when you can overtalk what your ancestors have said and done and not get into trouble because they aren't here to hear you, and you are in Christ, nothing can hurt you. Speak the Word and the Will of God, even if you had evil ancestors who did the opposite.

Works

The kingdom of heaven suffers violence and the violent take it by force. (Matthew 11:12)

Stating what you allow or disallow in your family and bloodline by your works is Godly. It is binding and *loosing*. It is spiritual warfare.

Now, we are not saved by works, we are saved byGrace and it is the gift of God, lest any man should boast.

For by grace are ye saved through faith; and that not of yourselves: it is the gift of God: Not of works, lest any man should boast. (Ephesians 2:8-9)

We do works for here, for now, for our family, our bloodline, our community, nation and world. Amen. We are to bear good fruit and fruit that remains (John 15:16). We are to do works because Christians will be judged in the White Throne Judgment not by whether we are saved or not. If you make it to the White Throne then you are saved, that's how you got there. The judging of the *works* whether it be hay, wood or stubble – whether it will burn because it will be tried by Fire is what that judgment is about.

Now if any man build upon this foundation gold, silver, precious stones, wood, hay, stubble;

Every man's work shall be made manifest: for the day shall declare it, because it shall be revealed by fire; and the fire shall try every man's work of what sort it is. (1 Corinthians 3:12-13)

For those who want to wait until the last minute (they think) to get saved because they think they are having fun the rest of the time. I ask those people, When do you plan to do *works*? – not just any works, but what GOD put you here to do? Good works and works that bear fruit that remains? When do you plan to do that? When will you work toward destiny?

How will the fruit of your womb or of your loins be good fruit if you don't protect them by binding and *loosing*, for example, by protecting them spiritually? How do you think you can do any old thing, live the party life and your children will grow up Godly? No, your children will take partying to the next level. They will be far worse than you. Far worse. They may start sooner, and they may go deeper into what they call the party life. You may be amazed at what the devil can get them to do because YOU opened the door and let those devils in. Now, if you are not still hosting the devils, praise God. Have you fully repented to God, or are you just acting like you've been holy all your life.

True story: A woman had eight kids before she ran off with another man and left those kids. Now that she is older, the first husband is dead, the man she ran off with and married is also gone, now this woman has reprogrammed her own memory and rewritten history of what a wonderful parent she was when she left every child with their birth father, her first husband. Revisionist history is a thing. But do you think this woman has repented? Of course not, she's not even saved. If she had repented she wouldn't be lying about what really happened. Repenting doesn't change what happened, it just absolves us of sin and erases iniquity. It doesn't give us permission to start lying that we never did what we actually did.

Her eight adult children all struggle to stay in marriages because of the doors she opened, and without repentance, those doors remain open. They are still open because she was the authority figure in that house over those kids.

The children? They are *fruit*, for sure and good or bad, fruit remains, else the Word wouldn't have specified, GOOD Fruit.

Saying you're saved and really being saved--, fantastic. Where are your _works_? What will you tell God when He says, Present your works. If you don't, your children will be seen as your works in the third and fourth generation *visits*. Without Christ, your kids and grandkids will look like YOU, spiritually.

Your New House

So, you have keys. Did you use those keys – most assuredly everyone does. They use the authority that they've been gifted for good or for evil. *How* did you use those keys? Yes, they are the keys to the good things that God has for your life.

How you live, binding and *loosing*, they are the keys to your house, your new house, your better house, your bigger house. They are the keys to the house of your family, the house of ____ whatever your last name is. They are the keys to a successful bloodline. Those are the keys to everything else that pertains to life, godliness and to your peace. Those are the keys to the Kingdom of Heaven. Whatever you bind on Earth will be bound in Heaven. Whatever you *loose* on Earth will have also been *loosed* in Heaven. What did you bind and *loose* all your life—up to this point? Whatever you have bound and whatever you have *loosed* – That is what got spiritually imprinted on the slate or the foundation of those that will come after you. Yes, they want to see you as a role model, setting a good example for their eyes, yeah, that's important.

But making your bold statements in the spirit, naming that which is good. Discerning and discarding that which is bad is what will impact those in your bloodline who may never see you in the natural, who may never meet you in the Earth realm, but who will be reaping from your binding and *loosing* – by your spiritual prescriptions. unless and until they meet Christ for themselves and begin their own Godly binding and *loosing*.

Don't make your kids have to start in a behind position or at a deficit in life because you did nothing or you did the wrong thing. (More in the book: **Living For the NOW of God**, by this author. https://a.co/d/7gSpmhC)

Keys Are Power & Authority

Jesus has keys and we have keys. Jesus has the keys to hell and death.

I am he that liveth, and was dead; and, behold, I am alive for evermore, Amen; and have the keys of hell and of death. (Revelation 1:18)

You have keys for binding and *loosing*. You have keys because you are in Christ, (Matthew 16:19, Mark 18:18) life and death are in the power of the tongue. (Proverbs 18:21)

Jesus has keys; He can shut doors that no man can open, and He can open doors that no man can shut.

And the key of the house of David will I lay upon his shoulder; so he shall open, and none shall shut; and he shall shut, and none shall open. (Isaiah 22:22)

The House of David speaks of government. When you bind and *loose* you are participating in the government of your own life, in the life of your family, your children, your bloodline, and those who you pray for, with permission. Those who try to force things on people are witches, warlocks, wizards, and the like.

You are in Christ and you and I --, we all bind or *loose* all the time, all day, and all night. By our deeds, words, actions, even by our thoughts. Yes, sin begins in our thought life. This is why we must take our thought life captive, else it will try to take us captive.

We take those keys into our hands, and we are aware and present all the time and we take it seriously, making definite declarations as to what we will allow in our own lives as well as the lives of those who come after us. We are creating a proper foundation for our children and *children's* children. The foundation will govern, that is, it will speak what is allowed or disallowed in a person's life, until Jesus Christ is invited to override and change it.

With words and acts we invite blessings and good things into our lives and into our future. We are writing on that slate. We are writing in spiritual realms, by what we say, do, allow, disallow, by binding and loosing We have the power to create a future for our children and their children – we have keys.

With that authority what we do or don't do is written in the spirit and it stands. It lasts; it remains until repentance and spiritual expungement happens.

What we say or don't say stands, without renunciation or repentance, like writing on a chalk board (a slate board) but more permanent. That declaration – what we named a thing is written in the spirit at least to the third and fourth generation – maybe longer.

Sadly, sin usually feels good in the moment, and it can be addictive. If we liked sin and didn't repent, then we are technically calling sin good and we are allowing it into our lives and into the lives of our children and bloodline. Spiritual blindness can come by lies – when people think that sin is good, when it is not, then they don't know how to rightly judge, rightly divide and may from the start not hear the Holy Spirit. Discernment is either not present or not working in such a person.

A widowed father has three boys. He has taught those boys to be the wildest things on the planet. He thinks that's fun; he thinks it is love. He and the children sit and drink together; he gets drunk with his kids. They are of adult age now but we don't know when this started, but we know that this man brags about how much his children can drink. Yes, they sit at home or go out and get falling down drunk. What demons has he let into their lives? What demons will his grandkids, if he gets any, have to deal with? Monsters? Yes, this is how they are created, generationally.

These kids call sin good. Woe to those who call evil good. In addition, he has taught them to be sex addicts and sits and talks with them as if they are all 20-year-old idiots in a locker room. Woe to those who call evil good.

Once, I heard a demon exclaim through a man, You believe in all that? In God? He believes that believing in God is evil and not good. Woe to them that call good evil. That man was created by his own father; he is the second generation. He has children but they also don't believe in God. By the time something gets into the third generation, it's really in there.

If we don't know this or use this authority, what was the purpose of having keys?

Your New House

It is wise to start with the end in mind. In this way, we can clearly get the keys before we get the house because as God chooses foolish things to confound the wise, we can use the keys to build the house. We go to Proverbs and learn that by Wisdom the house is built. God built the world as we know it in six days and on the seventh, He rested, but what He did in those six days was the building of the house. God said; He prescribed and then it happened; it was done.

Like God with our deeds, words, and actions, and thoughts, we prescribe for our own lives and the lives of our children, family, and bloodline.

Wisdom was with God that whole time. Of course, Proverbs 8 is an amazing

84

chapter and should be studied out. But here is an excerpt from it that relates to what we are talking about here.

> The LORD possessed me in the beginning of his way, before his works of old.

> I was set up from everlasting, from the beginning, or ever the earth was.

> When *there were* no depths, I was brought forth; when *there were* no fountains abounding with water.

> Before the mountains were settled, before the hills was I brought forth:

> While as yet he had not made the earth, nor the fields, nor the highest part of the dust of the world.

> When he prepared the heavens, I *was* there: when he set a compass upon the face of the depth:

> When he established the clouds above: when he strengthened the fountains of the deep:

> When he gave to the sea his decree, that the waters should not pass his

commandment: when he appointed the foundations of the earth:

Then I was by him, *as* one brought up *with him*: and I was daily *his* delight, rejoicing always before him;

Rejoicing in the habitable part of his earth; and my delights *were* with the sons of men.

Now therefore hearken unto me, O ye children: for blessed *are they that* keep my ways.

Hear instruction, and be wise, and refuse it not.

Blessed *is* the man that heareth me, watching daily at my gates, waiting at the posts of my doors.

For whoso findeth me findeth life, and shall obtain favour of the LORD.

But he that sinneth against me wrongeth his own soul: all they that hate me love death.(Proverbs 8:22-36)

Through diligence, prayers, dedication, obedience, and other disciplines of the Faith we build what we need, what we have faith for, what God has appointed to us.

My book, **How to Build Houses** the subtitle is prophetic, ***And Dismantle Weapons*** because weapons will surely be formed or trained on anything you build, including your house. By house here, I mean the structure you live in as well as the House of ____ whatever is your last name: your bloodline.

Everything that is built either in the natural or in the spirit realm is built by faith. This book teaches that we must build up our faith and that assists in our creating and building.

But ye, beloved, building up yourselves on your most holy faith, praying in the Holy Ghost, (Jude 20)

Prayer Points

1. Lord, have Mercy on me, a sinner. If I am none of Yours give me a Godly sorrow and repentant heart for my sins. Lord, hear my confession and make me one of Yours.

2. Lord, fill me with Your Holy Spirit and let the Spirit of God help me in these prayers, in the Name of Jesus.

3. By the Word of God I receive the authority, the keys to the Kingdom of Heaven and the power to bind and *loose*, according to Mark 18:18, in the Name of Jesus.

4. As for me and my house, we will serve the Lord, (Joshua 24:15)

5. As for me and my house, Lord we bind all evil from having interface with our home, in the Name of Jesus.

6. We invite the Light and Love of God into our lives and into our house, in the Name of Jesus.

7. We separate ourselves from darkness stating that light has no communion with darkness, in the Name of Jesus.

8. Lord, set me and this family/bloodline in proper position and authority, in Christ Jesus, Amen. (Deuteronomy 28:1)

9. We hear and obey the Word of God so that we can declare that the blessings of the Lord will overtake me, my family, and this house, in the Name of Jesus. (Deuteronomy 28:2)

10. Lord, I am blessed in the city and in the field, in the Name of Jesus. (Deuteronomy 28:3)

11. Lord, I declare that I am blessed in the fruit of my body and the fruit of my labors, and that everything that I set my hands to shall prosper in the Name of Jesus.

12. Lord, I declare that my checking account, savings accounts, investments and retirement accounts are blessed in the Name of Jesus. (Deuteronomy 28:5)

13. Lord, I declare that my side hustle is blessed, and will prosper, in the Name of Jesus. (Deuteronomy 28: 5, 8, 12)

14. I declare that wherever I go, wherever I am, I am blessed. I allow these blessings into my life and into the life of my family and bloodline, in the Name of Jesus. (Deuteronomy 28:6)

15. I declare that the enemies of God, also my enemies will flee away from me and my House seven-fold, in the Name of Jesus (Deuteronomy 28:7)

16. Bless me, Lord; bless me, indeed, in the Name of Jesus.

17. Father, command the blessing upon me and my House, in the Name of Jesus.

18. Thank you, Lord for establishing me and giving me property, land, and houses, in the Name of Jesus. (Deuteronomy 28:8)

19. I declare I am the righteousness of God in Christ Jesus. Lord, establish me and my House as holy people unto You as we keep the commandments of the Lord and walk upright before You, in the Name of Jesus. (Deuteronomy 28:9)

20. Lord, let the enemies of God be afraid of me and my people, in the Name of Jesus. (Deuteronomy 28:10)

21. Thank You, Lord, there is abundance and no lack. Father, make me and my House plenteous in goods. We allow sufficiency and prosperity, and we disallow scarcity and lack, in the Name of Jesus. (Deuteronomy 28:11)

22. I allow success in business and career, in the Name of Jesus. As for me and my house I disallow failure, disappointments and hindrances, in the Name of Jesus. (Deuteronomy 28:11)

23. Lord, open Your Good treasure to me and my house, my bloodline, forevermore, in the Name of Jesus. Supply all of our needs according to Your riches in Glory, in the Name of Jesus. (Deuteronomy 28:12)

24. I declare Lord, by covenant that You have made me the head and not the tail, the first and not the last, above only and not below. I declare that I am not the prisoner nor the captive, in the Name of Jesus. (Deuteronomy 28:13)

25. We follow the commands of the Lord and hear His words and do not turn away from God, not to the left or the right, and we are blessed, in the Name of Jesus. (Deuteronomy 28:14-15)

26. We accept the blessings of the Lord God. I accept the blessings into my life and in the life of my family and into my generations, into my bloodline, in the Name of Jesus.

27. We allow blessings, we disallow all curses and cursings. All curses, return to sender, in the Name of Jesus.

28. We reject being cursed anywhere in the Name of Jesus. (Deuteronomy 28:16, 19)

29. We reject being cursed in finances, in the Name of Jesus. (Deuteronomy 28:17)

30. We reject every curse over family and children. My children are blessed and not

cursed, in the Name of Jesus. (Deuteronomy 28:18)

31. We are blessed in the land that we live on, in the Name of Jesus. (Deuteronomy 28:18)

32. We are blessed in all business endeavors, in the Name of Jesus (Deuteronomy 28:18)

33. We reject pestilence, desolation, corruption, cursing, vexation sent by the enemies of God. We reject loss and failure, in the Name of Jesus. (Deuteronomy 28:20, 21)

34. We reject sickness, disease, disorder and death, we embrace the Stripes of Jesus by Which we were healed, in the Name of Jesus.

35. We reject smiting consumption, fever, inflammation with extreme burning, blasting, mildew and the sword, in the Name of Jesus. (Deuteronomy 28:22)

36. We reject any of the diseases of the Egyptians including *emerods*, scabs, the itch or any disorder or disease that is incurable; with God, all things are

possible, in the Name of Jesus. (Deuteronomy 28:27)

37. We reject and disallow insanity, madness, dullness of mind or spirit, blindness, sudden terror, astonishment of heart, in the Name of Jesus. (Deuteronomy 28:28, 29)

38. We reject brassy heaven. We reject iron earth, in the Name of Jesus. (Deuteronomy 28:23)

39. We reject any dry rain the enemy would send, in the Name of Jesus. (Deuteronomy 28:24)

40. We reject defeat and we embrace success and victory, in the Name of Jesus. (Deuteronomy 28:25)

41. We reject dishonor in life or death, in the Name of Jesus. (Deuteronomy 28:26)

42. We reject all physical and spiritual oppression and embrace destiny helpers, benefactors, kinsman redeemers and Jesus Christ, in the Name of Jesus. (Deuteronomy 28:29)

43. We embrace marriages, good marriages, healthy marriages, fruitful and successful

marriages, in the Name of Jesus. (Deuteronomy 28:30)

44. We are a family that seeks knowledge and also Wisdom and understanding, in the Name of Jesus.

45. We are a family who walk in the spiritual gifts of the Lord, including discernment and we sharpen our discernment by reason of use, in the Name of Jesus.

46. In this family, (bloodline) we will know when to stand, when to fight, when to rest, and when to wait on the Lord, by hearing and by obedience to the Word of God.

47. We are a family that flees youthful lusts, in the Name of Jesus.

48. We disallow poverty, insufficiency, lack, hardship, in the Name of Jesus.

49. We embrace the abundant life that Jesus came for us to have, in the Name of Jesus.

50. We will be good and kind to one another, showing forth the Fruit of the Spirit--, not disrespecting father, mother, sister or

brother, or any relative, in the Name of Jesus.

51. We will not disrespect any child, orphan, widow, or oppressed person, in the Name of Jesus.

52. We have all things that pertain to life and to godliness and all things that pertain to our peace, in the Name of Jesus.

53. We are about Godly purpose and destiny, fulfilling the Will of Him who sent us, in the Name of Jesus.

54. Our name will not be cut off in the Earth, all to the praise of the Glory of God. Amen.

55. On the foundation on which we've started we will build this House--, the House of _____ (whatever your last name is) so that God can tabernacle with us and He will have a place to dwell, in the Name of Jesus.

56. We build houses in the natural in our bloodline, and we live in them and we enjoy them, in the Name of Jesus. (Deuteronomy 28:30)

57. We plant and we reap from what we plant, in the Name of Jesus. (Deuteronomy 28:30)

58. The fruits of our labors are not abated, in any way, in the Name of Jesus. (Deuteronomy 28:31, 33)

59. We reject disorders and diseases of youth or old age, in the Name of Jesus.

60. We reject senior moments, arthritis of any kind, we reject being afflicted in the knees, legs, or hips, in the Name of Jesus. (Deuteronomy 28:35)

61. We reject and disallow the sore both that cannot be healed anywhere on or in the body, in the Name of Jesus. (Deuteronomy 28:35)

62. We declare that we age gracefully, rejecting all incurable or terminal diseases, in the Name of Jesus.

63. We declare that in Christ we shall be appreciated and esteemed, not mocked, ridiculed, made a cautionary tale, or made fun of, in the Name of Jesus. (Deuteronomy 28:37)

64. In multiplying, I declare that the Lord will multiply me, my family, and bloodline, in the Name of Jesus.

65. We plant much and we harvest much, to the Glory of God, in the Name of Jesus. (Deuteronomy 28:38)

66. We reject the locust, the cankerworm, the palmerworm, and any evil thing in my life, in the life of my family, or in the lives of our bloodline, in the Name of Jesus.

67. Thank, You, Lord for giving us the works of our hands and allowing us to enjoy it. We plant our vineyards and dress them and enjoy the wine thereof. Lord, let us share with our neighbors under the shade of our own trees, in the Name of Jesus. (Deuteronomy 28:39)

68. In this family we beget sons and daughters, and we enjoy our family, in the Name of Jesus. (Deuteronomy 28).

69. Strangers among us shall not be greater than we are, in my life, in my family, and in my bloodline, in the Name of Jesus. (Deuteronomy 28:43)

70. We shall not need to borrow but we shall be able to lend, in the Name of Jesus. (Deuteronomy 28:43, 44)

71. Lord, redeem me and my bloodline from serving our enemies, in the Name of Jesus.

72. We reject servitude to evil and to enemies, in the Name of Jesus.

73. We receive the strength to not be defeated by evil nations, in the Name of Jesus. (Deuteronomy 28:48-50)

74. We, by the power in the Christ of God, turn anything that is upside down, right side up again so that we're not walking while our servants are riding, in the Name of Jesus.

75. We reject hunger and thirst in our bloodline, we are in Christ, Amen. (Deuteronomy 28:48)

76. We cast off every burden, every bondage, every yoke, that is not the portion for my life, my family's life, or my bloodline, in the Name of Jesus. (Deuteronomy 28:49)

77. This family receives the power to get wealth and to enjoy that wealth, to receive of the fruit of our businesses and career endeavors, in the Name of Jesus. (Deuteronomy 28:50)

78. Lord, let me and my family walk in divine authority to possess the gates of our enemies, in the Name of Jesus. (Deuteronomy 28:51-52)

79. We reject being candidates for any evil for the devil or any of his evil human agents, in the Name of Jesus. (Deuteronomy 28:54-55)

80. For myself, my family and my bloodline, Father, I prescribe no plagues, no sore sicknesses, no diseases of the Egyptians, no cleaving diseases or disorders (Deuteronomy 28:59, 60, 61)

81. We declare and prescribe that no sickness, plague, disease, disorder that is not named or yet to be named will come upon me, my family, or my bloodline, in the Name of Jesus. (Deuteronomy 28:61)

82. Father, I prescribe that no destroying diseases or disorders shall come upon

me, my family or my bloodline, as we honor and bless you and do the Will of the Word of God, Amen. (Deuteronomy 28:61)

83. In multiplying, Lord, multiply this family and this bloodline so that we are not cut off from the Earth, in the Name of Jesus. (Deuteronomy 28:62)

84. Lord, rejoice over us and multiply us in the land that You have given us, in the Name of Jesus. (Deuteronomy 28:63)

85. Lord, let this family and bloodline be known for possessing our possessions, in the Name of Jesus.

86. We reject scattering, we reject idolatry, we reject captivity, and loss. (Deuteronomy 28:64-66).

87. We reject desolation and embrace rejoicing in the day, every day the Lord has made. (Deuteronomy 28:67)

88. Lord, we will not go back into captivity or bondage or endure yokes, that is not the portion for my life or my family or bloodline, in the Name of Jesus. (Deuteronomy 28:68)

89. We bind all evil entities from working their mischief and evil works against me and my family, in the Name of Jesus.

90. We bind idolatry and we *loose* worship to God alone, in the Name of Jesus.

91. We bind all idols devils, demons, unclean spirits, fallen *spirits*, false *gods* and destroy their power against us, in the Name of Jesus.

92. We bind and remove all graven images and likenesses of devils, demons, fallen *spirits*, or false *gods* from our houses and our lives, in the Name of Jesus.

93. We take the Name of the Lord with honor and respect and never in vain, in the Name of Jesus.

94. We honor the Sabbath as unto the Lord, in the Name of Jesus.

95. We honor father and mother so that we may live long and it may be well with us, in the Name of Jesus.

96. We do not kill; we do not murder and we do not allow such to dwell in our own homes, in the Name of Jesus.

97. We do not commit adultery or fornicate.

98. We do not steal.

99. We do not lie or commit false witness against neighbors.

100. We do not covet, we do not allow jealousy, unforgiveness, bitterness, resentment, or any other work of the flesh, in the Name of Jesus.

101. We abstain from fornication and all illegal sex with anyone who is not our covenanted marriage partner, in the Name of Jesus. (Acts 15:20, 29; 1 Thessalonians 4:2-3)

102. We avoid fleshly lusts and that pertains to our speech, talk, appearances and places we go, in the Name of Jesus. (1 Peter 2:11)

103. We abstain from eating meats offered to idols, we abstain from eating or drinking blood, in the Name of Jesus. (Acts 15:20, 29)

104. As for me and this house we avoid every appearance of evil, in the Name of Jesus. We do not let our good be evil

spoken of, in the Name of Jesus. (1 Thessalonians 5:22)

105. Bad company corrupts good manners; we avoid troublemakers, in the Name of Jesus. (Romans 16:17)

106. We avoid jesting and profane and vain babblings, in the Name of Jesus. (1 Timothy 6:20)

107. We avoid foolishness and foolish questions and foolish answers in the Name of Jesus. (Titus 3:9, 2 Timothy 2:23)

108. We avoid foolish arguments, dissensions, anger and every other work of the flesh, in the Name of Jesus. (Titus 3:9)

109. Lord, let us awake to righteousness, in the Name of Jesus. (1 Corinthians 15:34)

110. Lord, help us to avoid mumbling, grumbling, complaining and bitterness, in the Name of Jesus.

111. This is the day that the Lord has made, let us rejoice and be glad in it, in the Name of Jesus. (Matthew 5:12)

112. We do not promote quarrels, and we are quickly reconciled to one another, in the Name of Jesus. (Matthew 5:24)

113. Lord, give us the Mind of Christ and let us walk in Wisdom, circumspectly and in the Spirit so we do not fulfill the lust of the flesh, in the Name of Jesus.

114. In my life and in this house, Lord, let us be merciful as the Lord is also merciful, in the Name of Jesus. (Luke 6:36)

115. We are thankful. (Colossians 3:15)

116. We are faithful to God and one another. (Luke 12:36)

117. Lord, I declare that this house is a house of peace; those that dwell here dwell according to knowledge and to peace, in the Name of Jesus. (1 Thessalonians 5:13)

118. Lord, let the Fruit of the Spirit be evident in my life and in my dwelling place, in the Name of Jesus. (Galatians 5:23)

119. This is a house where prayer goes forth; it is a house of prayerfulness, not carelessness or dry Christianity, in the Name of Jesus. (1 Peter 4:7)

120. We have respect in the marriage of this house, husbands and wives are respected, in the Name of Jesus. (Titus 2:4)

121. Be patient in tribulation (Romans 12:12)

122. Let us be given to hospitality Lord, as many have entertained angels, unaware.

123. Lord, help us to be steadfast, unmovable, unshakeable, fully established and abounding in the Truth and the things of God, in the Name of Jesus. (1 Corinthians 15:58)

124. We do not embrace or have communion with darkness, in the Name of Jesus. We come out from among the unclean and the evil, in the Name of Jesus. (2 Corinthians 6:17)

125. Lord, let us be filled with the Spirit of God, in the Name of Jesus. (Ephesians 5:18)

126. Lord, let us teach our children at all times and let iron sharpen iron, in the Name of Jesus. (2 Timothy 2:24)

127. In my life and in this house let us maintain good works, let us bring forth fruit, good fruit, and fruit that remains, in the Name of Jesus.

128. In my life and in this house let me be a doer of the Word and not a hearer only, in the Name of Jesus. (James 1:22)

129. Lord, let me and those of my bloodline occupy until You return, in the Name of Jesus.

130. Let us overcome by the Blood of the Lamb and the Word of our testimony, in the Name of Jesus.

131. Thank You Lord, for hearing and answering prayers. We count it as done, in the Name of Jesus. Amen.

132. We will be watchful. Lord, help us to strengthen ourselves, in the Name of Jesus. (Revelation 3:2)

133. Lord, help us to be zealous and always repentant, in the Name of Jesus. (Revelation 3:19)

AMEN.

134. I seal these words decrees, declarations and prayers across every dimension and timeline, past, present, and future, to infinity, in the Name of Jesus.

135. I seal them with the Blood of Jesus and the Holy Spirit of Promise.

136. Any retaliation against this author, the reader or anyone who prays these prayers, makes these decrees and declarations at any time, let that retaliation backfire on the head of the perpetrator to infinity and without Mercy, in the Name of Jesus.

AMEN.

Dear Reader

Thank you for acquiring and reading this book, and supporting this ministry.

I pray this book has helped you tremendously to realize the power and the authority you have in Christ. I pray you receive, take up and use the keys of binding and *loosing* to establish your life, your family, your home, and your future.

As far as having a real home in the natural, these keys will help you build it, buy it, enjoy it and keep it, in the Name of Jesus. Amen.

Shalom,

Dr. Marlene Miles

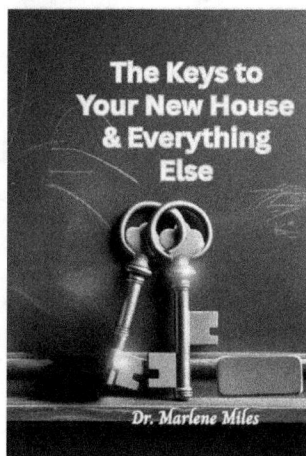

The Keys to Your New House & Everything Else

Dr. Marlene Miles

Links:

Repentance
https://www.youtube.com/watch?v=RogSEp2zH9o&t=66s

Mercy
https://www.youtube.com/watch?v=97DHnafJz6U

Dedicate Your Home
https://www.youtube.com/watch?v=9A66HDQGfLI&t=1686s

Heal My Foundation
https://www.youtube.com/watch?v=UkJs7HnJfNk&t=12s

Prayerbooks by this author

While most books by this author have prayer points either throughout the book or at the end, there are some books that are only prayers. You just open up the book and pray.

Prayers Against Barrenness: *For Success in Business and Life*

Fruit of the Womb: *Prayers Against Barrenness*

Beauty Curses, *Warfare Prayers Against* https://a.co/d/5Xlc20M

Courts of Marriage: Prayers for Marriage in the Courts of Heaven *(prayerbook)* https://a.co/d/cNAdgAq

Courtroom Warfare @ Midnight *(prayerbook)* https://a.co/d/5fc7Qdp

Demonic Cobwebs *(prayerbook)*
https://a.co/d/fp9Oa2H

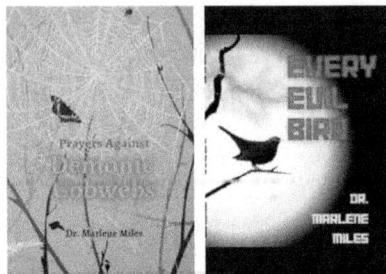

Every Evil Bird https://a.co/d/hF1kh1O

Gates of Thanksgiving

I AM NOT YOUR TARGET: *Warfare Against Haters & the Powers They Employ*

Spirits of Death, Hell & the Grave, Pass Over Me and My House

Throne of Grace: Courtroom Prayer

Warfare Prayer Against Poverty
https://a.co/d/bZ61lYu

Other books by this author

AK: The Adventures of the Agape Kid

Already Married in the Spirit: *Why You May Not Be Married in the Natural*

AMONG SOME THIEVES
https://a.co/d/dkYT4ZV

Ancestral Powers

Anti-Marriage, *The Spirit of*

Backstabbers https://a.co/d/gi8iBxf

Barrenness, *Prayers Against*
https://a.co/d/feUltIs

Battlefield of Marriage, *The*

Beware of the Dog: Prayers Against Dogs in the Dream.

Bless Your Food: *Let the Dining Table be Undefiled*

Blindsided: *Has the Old Man Bewitched You?* https://a.co/d/5O2fLLR

Break Free from Collective Captivity

Broken Spirits & Dry Bones

By Means of a Whorish Father

Casting Down Imaginations

Churchzilla, The Wanna-Be, Supposed-to-be Bride of Christ

Demonic Cobwebs (prayerbook)

Demonic Time Bombs

Demons Hate Questions

Devil Loves Trauma, *The*

Devil Weapons: Unforgiveness, Bitterness,...

The Devourers: Thieves of Darkness 2

Discernment: The Unabridged Guide

https://a.co/d/aaXdgnI

Do Not Swear by the Moon

Don't Refuse Me, Lord (4 book series)

https://a.co/d/idP34LG

Dream Defilement

The Emptiers: *Thieves of Darkness, 1*
https://a.co/d/5I4n5mc

Evil Touch

Failed Assignment

Fantasy Spirit Spouse
https://a.co/d/hW7oYbX

FAT Demons (The): *Breaking Demonic Curses* https://a.co/d/4kP8wV1

The Fold (5-book series)

- The Fold (Book 1)
- Name Your Seed (Book 2)
- The Poor Attitudes of Money (3)
- Do Not Orphan Your Seed (4)
- For the Sake of the Gospel (5)
- My Sowing Journal

Gang Ups: Touch Not God's Anointed

Getting Rid of Evil Spiritual Food

https://a.co/d/i2L3WYQ

got HEALING? Verses for Life

got LOVE? Verses for Life

got HOPE? Verses for Life

got money? https://a.co/d/g2av41N

Here Come the Horns: *Skilled to Destroy*
https://a.co/d/cZiNnkP

Hidden Sins: Hidden Iniquity

https://a.co/d/4MthOwa

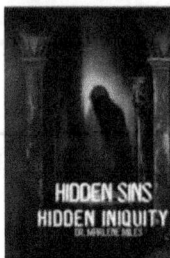

How to Build Houses: *And Dismantle Weapons* https://a.co/d/4gEU57y

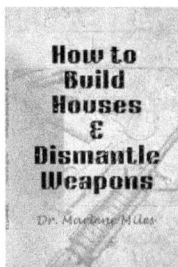

How to Dental Assist

How to Dental Assist2: Be Productive, Not Wasteful

How to STOP Being a Blind Witch or Warlock

I AM NOT YOUR TARGET: *Warfare Against Haters and the Powers they Employ*

I Take It Back

Keepsakes or Mistakes:

Keys to Your New House: *And Everything Else*

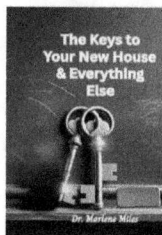

Legacy

Let Me Have A Dollar's Worth
https://a.co/d/h8F8XgE

Level the Playing Field

Living for the NOW of God
https://a.co/d/7gSpmhC

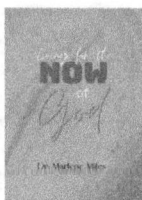

Lose My Location
https://a.co/d/crD6mV9

Love Breaks Your Heart

Made Perfect In Love

Mammon https://a.co/d/29yhMG7

Man Safari, *The*

Marriage Ed. Rules of Engagement & Marriage

Made Perfect in Love

Money Hunters: Beware of Those

Money on the Altar https://a.co/d/4EqJ2Nr

Mulberry Tree, *The*
https://a.co/d/9nR9rRb

Motherboard (The) - *Soul Prosperity Series*

Name Your Seed

Occupy: *Until I Return*
https://a.co/d/bZ7ztUy

Plantation Souls

Players Gonna Play

Portals: Shut the Front Door: Prayers to Close Evil Portals.

Power Money: Nine Times the Tithe

https://a.co/d/gRt41gy

The Power to Get Wealth
https://a.co/d/e4ub4Ov

Powers Above

The Robe, Part 1, The Lessons of Joseph

The Robe, Part II, The Lessons of Joseph

Seasons of Grief

Seasons of Waiting

Seasons of War

Second Marriage, Third~~, *Any Marriage*

https://a.co/d/6m6GN4N

Seducing Spirits: Idolatry & Whoredoms

https://a.co/d/4Jq4WEs

Shut the Front Door: *Prayers to Close Portals* https://a.co/d/cH4TWJj

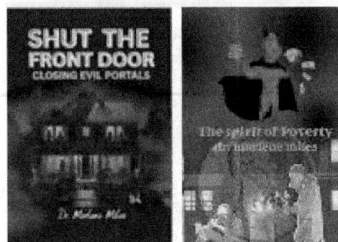

Sift You Like Wheat

Six Men Short: What Has Happened to all the Men?

SLAVE

Soul Prosperity soul prosperity series 3

https://a.co/d/5p8YvCN

Souls Captivity soul prosperity series 2

The Spirit of Anti-Marriage

The Spirit of Poverty
https://a.co/d/abV2o2e

Spiritual Thieves https://a.co/d/eqPPz33

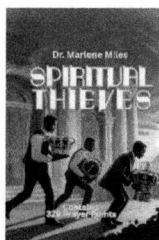

StarStruck~ Triangular Power series.

SUNBLOCK~ Triangular Power series.

The Swallowers: *Thieves of Darkness*, 3

Take It Back

This Is NOT That: How to Keep Demons from Coming at You

Time Is of the Essence

Too Many Wives: *Why You Have Lady Problems*

Tormenting Spirits
https://a.co/d/dAogEJf

Toxic Souls

Triangular Power *(series)*

- Powers Above
- SUNBLOCK
- Do Not Swear by the Moon
- STARSTRUCK

Unbreak My Heart: *Don't Let Me Die*

Uncontested Doom

Unguarded Hours, *The*

Unseen Life, *The* https://a.co/d/h3B5yFM

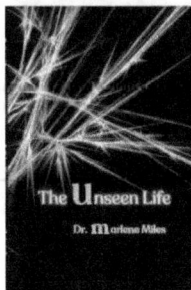

Upgrade: How to Get Out of Survival Mode

- Toxic Souls (Book 2 of series)
- Legacy (Book 3 of series)

The Wasters: *Thieves of Darkness*, Bk 2
https://a.co/d/bUvI9Jo

What Have You to Declare? What Do You Have With You from Where You've Been?

When I Was A Child, *I Prayed As a Child*

When the Devourer is Rebuked

https://a.co/d/1HVv8oq

The Wilderness Romance *(series)* This series is about conducting a Godly relationship and marriage with someone who is a Wilderness person. It is about how to recognize it and navigate through it. These books are about how not to get caught up in such.

- *The Social Wilderness*
- *The Sexual Wilderness*
- *The Spiritual Wilderness*

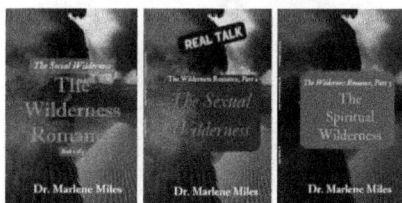

Other Series

The Fold (a series on Godly finances)
https://a.co/d/4hz3unj

Soul Prosperity Series https://a.co/d/bz2M42q

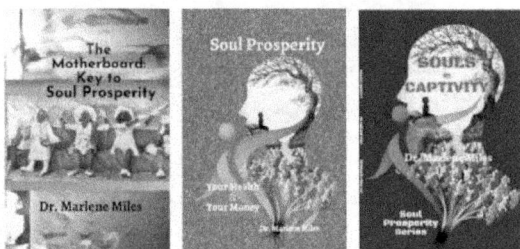

Spirit Spouse books

https://a.co/d/9VehDSo

https://a.co/d/97sKOwm

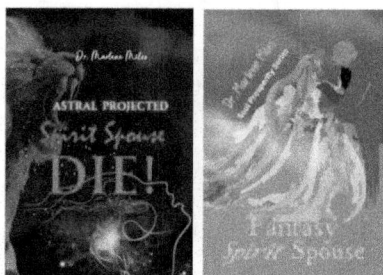

Battlefield of Marriage, The

https://a.co/d/eUDzizO

Players Gonna Play

https://a.co/d/2hzGw3N

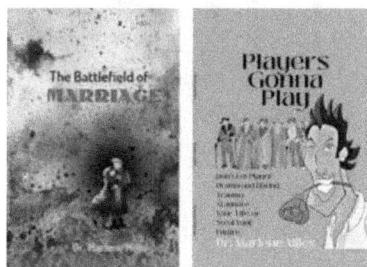

Sent Spirit Spouse (can someone send you a spirit spouse? This book is not yet released.)

Matters of the Heart

Made Perfect in Love
https://a.co/d/7OMQW3O

Love Breaks Your Heart
https://a.co/d/4KvuQLZ

Unbreak My Heart
https://a.co/d/84ceZ6M

Broken Spirits & Dry Bones
https://a.co/d/e6iedNP

Thieves of Darkness series

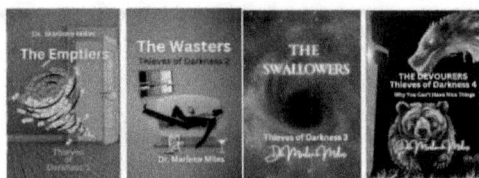

The Emptiers https://a.co/d/heio0dO

The Wasters https://a.co/d/5TG1iNQ

The Swallowers https://a.co/d/1jWhM6G

The Devourers: Why We Can't Have Nice Things https://a.co/d/87Tejbf

Spiritual Thieves

Triangular Powers https://a.co/d/aUCjAWC

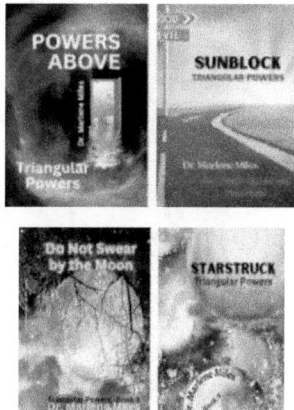

Upgrade (series) *How to Get Out of Survival Mode* https://a.co/d/aTERhXO

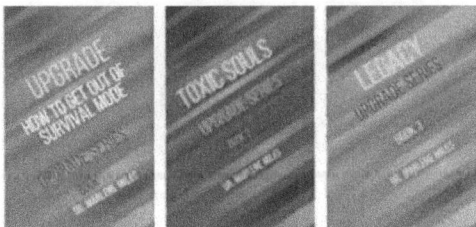

Notes

www.ingramcontent.com/pod-product-compliance
Lightning Source LLC
LaVergne TN
LVHW052031080426
835513LV00018B/2277